HOW TO WRITE YOUR WORST BOOK EVER

BREAK THROUGH THE FEAR, GET OVER YOURSELF, AND UNLOCK THE POTENTIAL WITHIN

BRADLEY CHARBONNEAU

REPOSSIBLE

PROLOGUE

This book came into existence because I, author guy with 30 books counting this one, hear this kind of thing so often:

"Oh, I'm working on a book, too. It's almost done. I just need another few years of research and to interview another 17 experts. Oh, and then I'll need to ... "

— PATRICIA "PERFECTIONIST" PARFAIT (GO.
REPOSSIBLE.COM/PARFAIT)

I used to talk with them and try to inspire them and help them. But I finally learned: they're probably never going to write that book. Or maybe they will. It's OK. I'm good with it. I hope they are.

I used to do the same thing. Talk about it, dream about it, but not actually do it.

For **years**.

Ouch.

Then there's this guy:

"Oh, you're an author? Yeah, I thought about writing a book.

But I went to dental school instead. You know, I did something real with my life."

— RITEOUS B. JELLOUS

They're pulling the old "Oh, you couldn't get a real job?" or even the "I'm better than you!" and maybe it's just me but I think they're possibly a little envious of the *artist* in an author. You see, I'm of the firm belief that there is an artist in all of us. **That artist within just needs to be unlocked.**

Smile and wave, boys, smile and wave. Just move on.

Or my personal favorite:

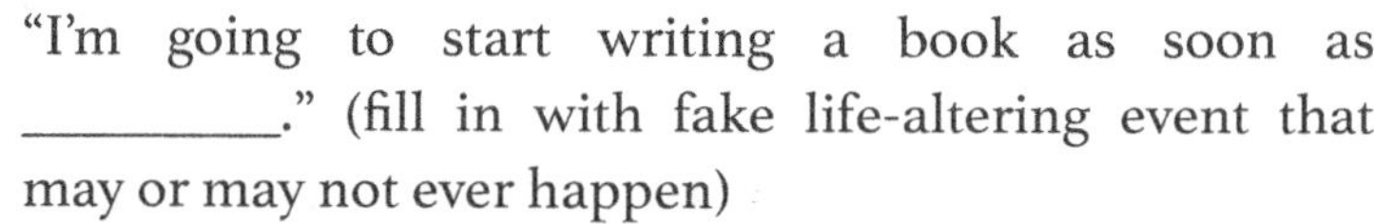

"I'm going to start writing a book as soon as ___________." (fill in with fake life-altering event that may or may not ever happen)

— PETE "PROCRASTINATION" PARDONHEIM (GO.
REPOSSIBLE.COM/PARDONHEIM)

I thought about putting together a book or course (or forced internment camp or cult compound or luxury resort holiday ...) where we wrote **Your Best Book Ever!**

Here's the syllabus:

1. **Solidify your idea** or story and scour the annals of the library of congress to be 100% certain no one has ever even mentioned such an idea. If you find mention of it, skip to Step #3 and then come back to Step #1. When (if ...) you ever find the idea/story, move to Step #2.
2. **Research the history** of the topic backwards and forwards, get a few university degrees in the topic (and related topics), and pen a few peer-reviewed, 300+ page documents on it that no one will ever read.
3. **Wait.** Just wait a while. (For the luxury resort retreat

version of the conference package, we might have to extend the hotel contract from "458 Days" to "This Side of Forever.") This part of the course is also called *procrastination*. It would be where most of the students go to perish. Maybe we could set up a hall where they could all go and share procrastination tips together. We'd provide bread, water, bathroom facilities, and pump "There's No Place I'd Rather Be" (by Pentatonix) through the ceiling speakers 24/7. I envision the future where there are hieroglyphics on the walls dug in with fingernails of not-very-soon-to-be authors along the lines of, "Tomorrow. I'll start tomorrow."

4. **Write.** Use ink pens. With the quills. Take your time. Grow a beard. Ponder. Sip hot drinks. Gaze.

5. **Edit.** Get the red pen. Cross out everything. Scribble in margins. Really lay on the criticism. Remember, we're heading towards the Valhalla of perfection. It's just around the next bend ...

6. **Find an agent.** Query only the top New York City literary agents. Send them hand-written letters by snail mail. If necessary, go back to Step #4 for a while.

7. **Sign contract.** But first, envision the fame, the fortune, the jet-setting life of rockstars. OK, now erase all that. Sign.

8. **Take a breath.** Wait, are you still breathing? Medic!

9. **Publish!** Your book is out in the world! Lean over from your hospice bed and scribble an autograph for the hordes of fans waiting outside your door. Oh wait. Those are medical personnel? They need the bed? Get back to celebrating! Try to do Step #8 more often, regularly. Like every 2 seconds.

10. **Repeat.** If that first book didn't go so well, just run through the steps again. No worries!

I didn't get *any* sign-ups!

Then I floated the idea of starting rather with **Your Worst Book Ever.**

This is what you have in your hands.

If you'd like to check out the **How to Write Your Best Book Ever** course, it's now free of charge here: go.repossible.com/bbe.

We'll get to this in the Mindset section but I think the book in us, the story in us, the artist in us (and don't forget, there's an artist in each and every single one of us) is whispering to be set free.

But that artist doesn't like perfection either.

They want to play.

They want happiness and joy and meaning and purpose.

They want to be let out of their cage and allowed to show the world what they have.

But in a light, fun, silly, *playful* way.

Because, dear reader, we are playful.

We want to play. It's part of us as humans.

Sure, we'll write that "best" book someday but we need to play first, to warm up, to stretch our imagination, and extend the boundaries of the fear that holds us back.

I might be a little biased and someone else might say you just need to get 8 years of therapy and eat blueberries.

I think it's possibly as easy as taking 10 days of your life and writing your worst book ever.

Or, you could start with Your Best Book Ever (no, really, it's here, it's totally free: go.repossible.com/bbe).

Up to you.

No, really, it's up to you.

And only you.

So there's that.

Welcome to How to Write Your Worst Book Ever.

FOREWORD

BY SARAH SIENKIEWICZ

> "No matter what your age or your life path, whether making art is your career or your hobby or your dream, it is not too late or too egotistical or too selfish or too silly to work on your creativity."
>
> — JULIA CAMERON, THE ARTIST'S WAY: A SPIRITUAL PATH TO HIGHER CREATIVITY

Writing your worst book ever - what a refreshing concept!

As an aspiring author who never seems to find the time to join challenges to write the "best book ever"- writing the worst book in a week felt strangely inviting! Possible even. And silly. Really silly. Suddenly, I discovered I did have the time to write.

At the live challenge, I met rebellious authors, like me, who enjoy a bit of disruption. It was reassuring to know I wasn't the only one harbouring a dream to write and yet sitting on a book idea, buried under a mountain of procrastination and perfectionism. For years. Can you relate? How long have you been planning on writing your "best" book, but never quite making the time for it?

Coming together as a community, playing with words, encouraging each other to laugh, be silly, and have a lot of fun took all the suffering out of writing. We finished a book in a week- how amazing is that?! (Suffering is optional if you enjoy that kind of thing).

Bradley can show you how to structure a book and the technical aspects of putting it together which is invaluable - and almost like a by-product of the "worst book" experience. You'll come away with so much more than simply a finished book.

Writing your worst book is like when your creativity is allowed to run free, unbound by pressure and performance anxiety. Dance like no one's watching, sing like no one's listening, and write like it's the worst book ever. It's the key to self-expression and tapping into your infinite reservoir of joy for joy's sake. This book can help you to take yourself and your art less seriously. If you're anything like me, you may even find you rekindle your love for writing and devotion to your craft through Bradley's process. Prepare to have fun, unlock fresh ways of thinking, and most importantly, be very, very silly.

Sarah Sienkiewicz
Worst Book Alumni
March 21, 2021
go.repossible.com/sarah

INTRODUCTION

There's an exercise in the Worst Book Ever challenge where we write our own worst reviews.

It can be a little painful. Sometimes, it really hits home and it hurts.

But it's like a Band-Aid, we rip it off, it hurts, but the sting goes away quickly.

The thing is, however, that the one-star review exercise comes from deep within. We are often so scared not only of what others think but what WE think of our own work.

Which is why, again and again, I'll keep saying, "Remember, this is your worst book ever! It's supposed to be terrible!"

But here in the introduction to this book, before you even start, I'm going to arm the enemy, I'm adding fuel to the fire, I'm digging my own grave.

OK, it sounds melodramatic but wait until you get to the chapter called "Take Away Their Ammunition" and you'll see what I mean.

So here goes, 1-star for THIS book, yep, the one you're reading and yes, I'm doing this before the book even starts, before you even start reading because that's just the way we do things here at WBE Inc.

 "Worst Book Ever? Well, the author sure got the title right!"

— S.C. JOHANNSON (NOT-QUITE-YET AUTHOR)

See what happened there? I go straight for the heart and dish out the pain!

 "Wait a minute here! This book is nothing more than a devious ploy to get the reader to join the Worst Book Ever 10-Day Challenge! 1-star!"

— SANFORD MCSLEUTH, PRIVATE EYE

Sometimes, 1-star reviews have a smidgen of truth in them. This book is exactly that and I'm stating it right here, right now, before you even go further in this book. Yep, this book will give you lots of the tools you need to write your own Worst Book Ever, but when you get to the section called TriTiTo, you might just want to join the next challenge.

See how easily I "diffused" that potentially awkward situation? What if you thought what Sanford did and wrote a review or contacted me, the author, about it and said, "Wait a minute!" and then I could say, "Yep, oh, do you mean that part in the introduction where I said the book was a devious ploy to get you to join the challenge?" Yep, that's fair.

The 3-Star Reviews

As an author, I am more weary of the 2- or 3-star reviews. The 1-star reviews are often from angry people who are, well, just angry in general and they write bad book reviews and can even give a can of kidney beans a 1-star spew of anger.

But those 2- and 3-star ones? They put some thought into it. Ready to watch this author completely annihilate himself in his own book? Watch this.

> "OK, I have to hand it to the author for his creativity in breaking through people's limiting beliefs in such a fun and unique way. The whole concept has really got me thinking. But then he's going to tease us and tell us that this whole process would be better in a group setting with other like-minded soon-to-be authors and we all do it together over a fixed time period? I mean, come on! It's brilliant, sure, but couldn't he at least give us a discount to the challenge if he's going to spend this whole book leading us to the slaughter? 3 stars!"
>
> — GUNTER B. RIGHTEN, SPEAKER OF TRUTH (AND FUTURE WBE ALUM)

Dear Reader,

As you may have noticed, this isn't your average book. I'm also not your "average" author. I mean, Jiminy Cricket, I have a one-word book published!

So yes, I'm coming clean: this book could (and should!) help you get over the fear and write your worst book ever.

But it's also an invitation to join the 10-Day Worst Book Ever Challenge.

Yep, it costs money.

Yep, this book is leading to that challenge.

Yep, I'm telling you this in advance.

Because I don't have any (OK, many ...) secrets.

I'll even give you the steps that are the foundation of the entire challenge right here:

1. Get Over Yourself
2. Write
3. Publish

I feel like I got something off my chest. You?

Full Disclaimer: Yep, as I just said, this book could lead you to a paid online, group challenge run by me, Bradley. However, as with most of my books, my main goal with this book (and I hope it's worth the few bucks you maybe spent on it) is to challenge you, to inspire and motivate you, to NOT suffer for 9 years of my life NOT daring to do the things that I was pretty sure I wanted to do. That's it, that's my big secret mission. #noregrets

PART I

WAIT, WHAT?

INTRO TO THE INTRODUCTION

I endlessly make fun of my nieces when they don't understand something because they always say the same thing.

Then I go ahead and repeat that question because I like being the complete dork uncle that I am.

They ask, with a look of puzzlement in their eyes and a blank stare.

"Wait, what?"

1

WORST. WAIT A MINUTE. YOU MEAN BEST, RIGHT?

WELL, YES, EVENTUALLY BUT ... THERE'S MORE TO IT

 "Don't let schooling interfere with your education."

— MARK TWAIN

I know, I know, you, dear soon-to-be author, want to write your Best Book Ever.

We'll get to that.

But first, we just have to do this one little thing.

We have to break through a tiny little barrier.

Open the flood gates.

Crush the wall.

Yes, of course, we have only one thing, or rather one person, we need to overcome, to get over, to laugh with, for, and at.

You.

No, really. This is what the Worst Book Ever means.

I joke around. No, a lot. I have witty book titles that no one understands ("Pass the Sour Cream"), I named companies I founded after small islands in obscure corners of Africa ("Likoma"), and now I write a book and am leading a 10-day challenge called "How to Write Your Worst Book Ever."

I'd like to get the facts out there first and foremost as we start this book. Just so we're clear.

Yes, this is a book about writing your worst book ever.

Key words to pay attention to:

1. **Writing:** yep, we'll do a smidgen of writing (no, really, not much)
2. **Your:** it's not THE worst book ever. It's YOUR worst book ever. PRO TIP: your next book will be better, almost guaranteed.
3. **Ever:** this is a bit of a twist here because chances are good that it will be your FIRST book so, by definition, it's also your WORST book. Also by definition, it's your BEST book. Funny, right? See point #2 about improving.

This book stems from a 10-day challenge we have run where people, together in a group, meet online for 10 days and write a (very!) short, very terrible book together. They Get It Done.

The trick? The secret? The grand finale?

It's really about breaking through, it's about learning new "definitions" of what a book means to you, getting over your serious self, having fun, goofing around, meeting new people, sharing your stories (on paper and online and on our Zoom calls), and going out of your comfort zone for 10 days.

Book vs. Challenge

Again, just trying to be transparent here. This is a book, yep, the one you have in your hands. There's everything you need to write a (bad) book in 10 days.

The challenge is a 10-day, online, group focused, real-time, challenge to write a short book in just those days and get it done by the end.

There's also a DIY version where you don't have to be together with a group if you don't want or need to.

There's more about the challenge throughout the book and there's a coupon to join us at the end of this book.

So...

Wait, what?

Let's just jump in.

We learn by doing.

Repossible

- **Possible:** best
- **Impossible:** best first
- **Repossible:** worst first

P.S. This book comes under the umbrella of the Repossible brand. A multi-book series, school, and community. The subtitle for the brand is "Who Will You Be Next." One of the books in the series is called "Create" and it's about taking action, making, doing, creating something. Maybe writing something. This book in your hands is an answer to readers who asked me, "Bradley, I am a believer now. I know I should create. Yay me! But WHAT should I create? How do I start?"

P.P.S. In those books, I have this little list at the end of each chapter Possible, Impossible, and Repossible. You could see it as Easy, Hard, Best. Or maybe Tomorrow, Yesterday, Today. See how it works? I'm going to use after each chapter in this book.

PART II

METHODOLOGY

YOU'RE NOT GOING TO LEARN HOW TO WRITE. YOU'RE GOING TO LEARN HOW TO THINK.

I guess it's a bit like the "meth" from "methamphetamine" but *methodology* is far more powerful and equally addictive when you get it in the right dose.

2

——————

MADNESS AND THE METHOD
THERE'S A METHOD TO THE MADNESS

"My goal is simple. It is a complete understanding of the universe, why it is as it is and why it exists at all."

— STEPHEN HAWKING

One might say:

"I'm supposed to write the worst book ever? Oh, that's easy. I'm just going to write blah blah blah and then copy that and paste it 14,000 times and call it a book."

— ONE

Yep, I suppose one could do that.

But we wouldn't learn anything from it.

The Worst Book Ever isn't going to be a course in grammar, spelling, and plot theory. In fact, we teach as little about "writing" as possible.

The "methodology" is more aligned with mindset, getting it done, working together in a group, and celebrating the successes.

Yep, you could go it alone. Yep, we could make the WBE challenge just some online course you do at your leisure. It could work.

But there is theory, experience, and, yep, even a methodology to the madness.

This section of the book explores the methods used in WBE and why we use them.

Repossible

- **Possible:** blah blah blah for 48 pages
- **Impossible:** learn from copying and pasting
- **Repossible:** merge the methodology with the madness

3

SNL

HEROIN AM

"For people who want to do heroin, but also be productive, there's Heroin AM."

— SATURDAY NIGHT LIVE

The Saturday Night Live (SNL) skit is one of my favorite sources of comedy, wit, and satire. In fact, it's one of the models we strive to emulate at WBE HQ.

If you analyze what they're doing—and how they're doing it—they take everyday topics and spin them to make them ridiculous or focus in on one particular aspect and blow it out of proportion so much that it becomes completely silly—but also memorable, fun, and usually brilliantly clever.

Even the (meta) concept of Worst Book Ever comes from the modeling of an SNL skit.

"Struggling to write brilliant prose? Just write complete garbage!"

"Forget the best-seller list, we're riding atop the worst-seller list!"

"Beat the critic to the punch with your own 1-star slams!"

The SNL skit model isn't the only way to write your WBE but it's certainly a fun one.

Plus, and this is a huge plus, if you manage to twist your topic in a way that you can still get your point across while making light of the situation, and get that reader (or viewer) to **smile** AND **remember** it, you're far ahead of the pack who are struggling with Chapter One of their Best Book Ever.

Where, of course, they're stuck staring at the blank page.

But the cherry-on-top, extra-bonus, dance-remix-version of the entire WBE concept is if you can actually put your WBE to (good) use.

A quick example.

The Breakfast of Losers

In case that reference is lost on you, it comes from an old ad for cereal (I can't even remember which one) called "The Breakfast of Champions."

I had a nutritionist in a summit I was hosting and she was talking about **the book she wasn't writing**, something about the best breakfast you can have to boost your morning energy, balance your mood throughout the day, and keep you going until afternoon.

Did you catch that bolded part? The most important part?

The book she **wasn't** writing.

Why not? Oh, let us count the ways:

1. "I'm not really such a great writer."
2. "There are people more expert than me out there on the subject."
3. "Who would read it?"

4. "There are probably so many other books out there on the topic."

The killer part? She's probably right about most if not all of them. So what to do?

The SNL Skit

As we talked about the WBE, I noticed this professional woman lighten up a bit. I could tell she was no longer really paying attention to our conversation because her mind and her imagination were racing with the idea of her own WBE.

She interrupted me and said:

> "Oh, wait, I know. I could have the worst breakfast! It could be the breakfast to get you off to a sluggish start, put you on an emotional rollercoaster throughout the day, and end your afternoon in a puddle of tears."
>
> — FORMERLY VERY SERIOUS NUTRITIONIST

Are you following along here? Let's take the two scenarios:

1. **Best Book Ever:** she's not going to write it. It's intimidating, scary, and not-all-that-much-fun.
2. **Worst Book Ever:** she's already having fun writing it before she's even started.

Which one is going to lead somewhere? ANYwhere? Which one is she actually, ever in her lifetime, going to do—and finish?

We came up with some great book titles. Oh, and this took us a matter of minutes, required hiring no professional book naming consultancy, was absolutely fun, and we laughed throughout.

Her Worst Book Titles Ever

- Start your day off wrong with the breakfast of losers!
- Impossible Recipes for Terrible Tasting Breakfasts that Will Make You Wish You Didn't Wake Up
- The Worst Breakfast You Can Put in Your Body Before 9 AM
- Breakfast: It's What's for Dinner

I just created those titles as I'm typing this chapter. We created more when we were on the phone together. If we put some thought into it, we could dig deeper into the real-life challenges that people have with breakfast (or consistent energy and/or mood throughout the day) and play with it, poke fun at it, and get people to do a double take.

Honestly here, if you saw two book covers on a nutritionist's website and one was a serious book about breakfast and the other was a parody, which would you choose?

It's just so bad, it's good.

These are the kinds of exercises we do in the WBE challenge.

See the full, "Heroin AM" 2-minute video here: go.repossible. com/heroin-am or find it in the WBE Bonus Content (go.repossible. com/wbe-bonus).

> "Would you like a little more heroin on your cereal, dear?"

Repossible

- **Possible:** try not to offend people who do heroin
- **Impossible:** stop all people from doing heroin
- **Repossible:** be productive AND do heroin AND poke fun at our realities

Oh, now I remember. It was Wheaties. The Breakfast of Champions.

4

———

FAIL FAST, FAIL OFTEN

IF IT WORKS FOR SILICON VALLEY, WE COULD AT LEAST GIVE IT A TRY

 "Test fast, fail fast, adjust fast."

— TOM PETERS

I didn't realize how much of an American concept this is—and even more so, a Silicon Valley mantra—until I moved to The Netherlands.

In the United States, especially in the start-up industry, it's almost a badge of honor that a company you founded completely tanked, went bankrupt, or died a slow and painful death.

"Congratulations!"
"What's next?!"
"Welcome to the club!"

I'm pretty sure I can state it as fact: we learn more from our failures than our successes.

When my son Luca's basketball team wins every game by 30, his team doesn't improve. They go through the motions, they think they're great (which they may or may not be), and they don't think about it, rehash the game, or learn a single thing.

But when they lose?

Analysis. Doubt. Questions:

"What did we do wrong?"

"Where can improve?"

"How can we not repeat the same mistakes?"

I think it's time for a quick math quiz. How about a word problem?

Speedy Sam

Speedy Sam has zillions of ideas for his business. He doesn't know which one to pick so he just begins with one and goes with it until it bombs, loses steam, or succeeds. They usually bomb—and they bomb quickly.

He's easy going about it, pulls himself up by the bootstraps, and tries the next thing. Then he hits gold and life is good, a project is a success!

> **Word Problem:** if Sam succeeds 10% of the time and he creates 1 new project per week, what is the maximum number of weeks possible before Sam has a winner?

> **BONUS:** how many projects can Sam successfully create in 1 year?

Steady Samantha

Steady Samantha is a thorough gal. She intensely researches each project before she even allows herself to think about moving forward. She holds meetings with her friends, strangers in the supermarket checkout line, and that old woman on bus #48 who might be deaf, and discusses and plans and strategizes about her upcoming projects.

She works with her team (Pete "Procrastination" Pardonheim (go. repossible.com/pardonheim) and Patricia"Perfectionist" Parfait (go. repossible.com/parfait) to create elaborate organizational charts and process maps of her future projects.

- **Word Problem:** if Samantha completes 0% of her projects every single day, 7 days a week, how many weeks will it take her to finish her first project?

- **BONUS:** if Samantha never actually begins a project, how many will she finish in a year?

- **DOUBLE CHOCOLATE BROWNIE BONUS:** if Samantha factors in 2 hours of therapy per month and her therapist, Melanie "Moonbeam" Millerton (go.repossible.com/ millerton), charges €100 per hour, how long before Samantha is sentenced to prison for the murder of Speedy Sam?

I think it's time to talk about gardening and architecture. I'll see you in the next chapter.

Repossible

- **Possible:** fail slowly
- **Impossible:** skip failure, succeed (on the first try and subsequently forever after)
- **Repossible:** fail fast, fail often

DEDICATION

To those of us who struggled and suffered, whined and moaned, tried and tormented, and thought it was true that we all must write a book.
And to those who dared take 10 days to write their Worst Book Ever and put an end to the torment, suffering, and whining about ... not having written a book.
And ... to the Bradley of October 31, 2012, who was scared, sad, and solitary in his quest to become a writer and didn't.
Yet.

"An essential aspect of creativity is not being afraid to fail."

— EDWIN LAND

CONTENTS

5

___

THE GARDENER AND THE ARCHITECT

THIS IS ABOUT AS CLOSE AS WE'RE GOING TO GET TO WRITING STYLE

 "All you need in this life is ignorance and confidence, and then success is sure."

— MARK TWAIN

Remember, in WBE, we are not going to teach you How to Write, How to Create the Best Plot Twists, how to spell, or even talk, much, about grammar.

Yet, we will happily discuss **what type of writer you might be**.

Let's drill down to the Trader Joe's option of two types of writers:

1. The Architect
2. The Gardener

The Architect

The architect uses a blueprint to build the house. She draws it up, measures twice, cuts once, and has it all laid out before she puts hammer to nail—or pen to paper.

Organized, methodical, structured.

The Gardener

The gardener sows seeds and sees what grows. It could be that the gardener doesn't even know which seeds she has in her hand and tosses them to the earth and it could become a sunflower, a beanstalk, or a redwood tree. The gardener has to first "do" and then learn and see and maneuver.

Stephen King is a famous gardener, he says he has to first write to get to know his characters before he learns what they're going to do in each book.

I'm a card-carrying gardener but I am learning the oh-so-sage ways of the architect. Even in writing this book and running the WBE challenge, I can't "teach" or "lead" or "guide" in the gardener ways,

"Go, be free, write until something falls from the heavens!"

Yeah, that's not going to go over very well.

So I have seen the rainbow at the end of the tunnel and I have a become a **gardener with a map.**

I mention these two types in the context of this WBE book and the challenge because my "issue" with architects is when they take 364 days to draw up the blueprints (or create an outline for the book) and then have 1 day left to write it. Oops.

So whereas I'm all for structure and maps and blueprints and outlines, especially in the case of the WBE, I want us to CREATE, to make, to fail, to do, because at the end of the challenge, there's one thing we're going to do that most architect and gardener authors alike rarely get accomplished: **we're going to finish our book.**

Which type of writer are you?

- Gardener
- Architect

Which type would you like to be?

- Gardener
- Architect

Repossible

- **Possible:** pretend you're the other when you know you're
  the other
- **Impossible:** map out exactly which seed will grow where
  and when and how and why
- **Repossible:** a gardener with a plan

Did you catch that mention of the word finish? It's a biggie.

6

____

FINISH

REMEMBER THE TORTOISE? HE WINS.

 "**Almost** is only worth something in horseshoes and hand grenades."

— AMERICAN SAYING

Even though I was a math major in college, it took me the longest time to figure out that the tortoise actually won.

In case you need refreshing on the math word problem, it went something like this:

> The tortoise and the hare are in a race to the finish line. The hare can run at speeds up to 50 kilometers per hour. The slowpoke tortoise muddles along at 2 kilometers per hour.

> The hare covers half of the distance to the finish line in each hour.

> The tortoise just goes 2 kilometers per hour.

> HINT: If the race were 1,000 kilometers, the hare would

already be at the 500-kilometer marker whereas the tortoise is only at the 2-kilometer point.

Who wins the race?

I remember mapping it out with a ruler and was sure that the hare would win.

> What a head start!
> What speed!
> Halfway to the finish on the first leap?
> The tortoise will never catch up!

But towards the end, it doesn't matter that the hare only has 0.0000001 millimeter to go, he NEVER finishes because each time, by definition, he only goes halfway to the finish line.

You know where I'm going with this.

- Book
- Excitement
- Writing
- Inspiration
- Motivation
- Pacing
- Procrastination
- Perfectionism
- Panic
- Halfway
- Dread
- Defeat

Wow. Yeah, that wasn't fun.

At the time you're reading this, I may or may not have finished a book in the Repossible series called Finish.

It's so important.

During the WBE challenge, some people would suddenly "get it," that lightbulb would go off above their heads and they'd say something like:

"Oh, now I get it, Bradley!

This whole WBE challenge is really about breaking through, about daring to start, overcoming our fears and creating something because then—and only then—will we learn from our mistakes and failures, gain clarity on what to do next and have the motivation and inspiration to then go and actually DO that next thing!

Yeah, so the challenge has been great but I'm going to stop now before I finish my WBE because I have seen the light, learned enough, and I'm ready for my Best _______ Ever."

— SOME WBE STUDENTS

To which I say:

"Yeah, so, uh, no."

— BIG BAD BRADLEY THE MEAN TEACHER

No.

In Worst Book Ever, we **finish** our books.

1. Bad title
2. Silly subtitle
3. Horrendous cover
4. Foreword (written by someone else)
5. Introduction (or prologue)
6. Chapters (how many is not important)
7. Epilogue
8. All together in a downloadable ebook format

Otherwise, it's the hare.

Halfway to the finish line.

But not quite.

At the end of the race, I want you to hold that book in your hands. It's symbolic, it's important, it's crucial in moving forward.

I know starting is hard—that's what we're doing with WBE. But finishing is less hard once you've started.

Repossible

- **Possible:** start
- **Impossible:** pretend you finished (and believe you did)
- **Repossible:** finish

PART III

TRITITO

TRIGGER TIME TOGETHER

The foundation, the framework, maybe even the magic formula behind what makes WBE work was found deep in the south American jungles. A man was chanting three syllables and as I approached him, he told me this was my mantra.

Or something like that.

7

***

FROM DEEP IN THE AMAZONIAN JUNGLE

THE FRAMEWORK TO MAKE IT ALL HAPPEN

 "The creative process is mysterious; a conversation, a ride in the car, or a melody can trigger something."

— ALEJANDRO GONZALEZ INARRITU

How do your ideas come to you? The small ones? The big ones?

For me, it's often during meditation. The best meditations are the ones where it just comes to you. "You just know."

I know, it's annoying to hear about that when it doesn't happen to you (or at least, doesn't happen as often as you'd like). For that challenge, I can offer this: surrender.

> Yes, it's true. I think in terms of books. Yep, often my own
> books. Have I mentioned the **trigger** yet?

Let's get back to the jungle.

Don't ask me how this comes about (and not because I won't tell you but because I just have no idea ... I just surrender and let it come to me) but there was this tribal dude deep in a rain forest.

You see, if I were to tell you these three syllables in my normal voice, coming from me, Mr. Kinda Sorta Normal Guy, and I told you here in a book and not even in person, much less not in some exotic locale like a jungle, it might mean less.

Thus, the scene. The backstory.

As I dig back deep into my dark and depressing past (that's pre-2012 for anyone keeping track) and I take the present moment and look back and try to figure out how I got from there to here, these three words came to me: **trigger time together.**

But then again, the jungle. The tribal guy.

Imagine, just go with me for a minute here, you're deep in the jungle and you're hacking the vines with your machete and wondering when a snake is going to drop onto your neck and .... OK, too much detail.

A friendly old warrior comes out from behind a tree the size of a skyscraper.

You're not sure he's going to kiss you, kill you, or offer you a potion made of dead beetle ankles.

He holds out his hands forming a cup as if there's a potion in there we're supposed to drink.

But we look in. It's empty.

He says in this guttural yet somehow song-song voice:

Tri Ti To

I want to say, "Uh, ex-squeeze me?"
But we say nothing.
He just says it again.

Tri Ti To

He says it so many times we can no longer ignore it.

I'm pretty sure I had worked out the "Trigger Time Together" before this meditation and the visit from the friendly jungle man but then he drove it home for me.

In any case, it's now my formula to decide whether or not to take on a project—and be able to predict its success.

Introducing TriTiTo.

Repossible

- **Possible:** don't listen to your dreams
- **Impossible:** try to find that guy in Brazil
- **Repossible:** listen to your dreams

You can see my video version of this post in the WBE Bonus Content, go.repossible.com/wbe-bonus.

8

———

TRIGGER

SOMETHING, OR SOMEONE, WILL INVITE YOU.
HOW WILL YOU ANSWER?

> "It will certainly not be the worst book ever since it's done. It'll be way better than only having the 'best book ever' in our mind. ;)"
>
> — WBE AUTHOR

The nutshell: what is going to start the action (that will cause the reaction)?

Are you the determined, stubborn, DIY, "I got this," and "I'll figure it out on my own and I don't need anyone else" kind of decision maker?

I sure was.

Let's do a little scoreboard:

- Books written with "I got this alone!" attitude: 0
- Books written with "We're better together!" mantra: 30

Ouch.

Don't get me wrong: I have accomplished tons on my own! No, really! I promise!

But the hard stuff? The real elements? The core dreams that will make me who I am?

Yeah, those I held close to the vest, in the closet, and all to myself.

I suffered through years of "dreaming the dream" and although I didn't realize it, I was waiting for someone to invite me to the real life I was pretty sure I was supposed to be living.

For me, it's simple: my trigger came in the form of a guy named John Muldoon in San Francisco in 2012.

Larkin Street on our way to a hole-in-the-wall Ethiopian café and I "came out of the writer's closet" and told John that I had been "working on" a novel.

I had worked with the guy for years and had never "bothered to mention that."

At the time, he was running a project called "Monthly Experiments" (Trigger) where, for just one month (Time), with a group of people (Together), you did something out of your comfort zone.

It was often:

- no caffeine
- wake up at 5 AM
- stop work at 5 PM

But on Larkin Street that fateful day in San Francisco, he set in motion the trigger that was about to change the rest of my life.

He set up a monthly experiment to "Write Every Day" for the month of November, 2012.

That was it.

Simple as a pimple.

The thing was, I actually did it.

I started on the 1st of November and I wrote until the 30th of November.

But what happened after those 30 days, and what John knew because he had "tricked" many people into learning habits through prior experiments, was that after those 30 days, I might say something like:

 "Gee, that wasn't as difficult as I thought it was going to be."

— MOST PEOPLE

I kept going. I ended up writing 2,808 days in a row without missing a day.

I published 30 books, I closed down my design agency, moved my family to Europe, and I'm now the writer I had dreamed about since I was 20 years old.

All from coming out of my shell on Larkin Street to a friend who took action and then **triggered** me to **take action**.

He invited me to do something I knew I wanted to do.

But apparently, I needed that instigation, that prodding, pulling, that little push to get me going.

I needed John Muldoon.

I needed a *trigger*.

Seemingly Insignificant

Was Larkin Street full of fireworks that day? Did I get struck by lightning? Champagne? Fanfare? Applause? Recognition?

Nope. Nada.

This might be the most important element of this book, of the WBE Challenge, of your upcoming life.

This trigger we're talking about here. This action that will, hopefully, cause a reaction.

It might not come in the form of magical sparkles and background music from your favorite dramatic Netflix series.

It's terribly possible that the Rolling Stones don't burst into the room where you're reading this book and bust out a tune that's going to catapult you into the future you've been wishing for.

There probably won't be cheering.

Possibly no mountain top screaming from the top of your lungs.

It might be subtle.

It could be practically invisible.

It's probably unexpected.

It's almost certainly going to happen soon.

If you're open to the invitation.

If you'll allow the answer to come along and respond to your question, to your calling, to who you will be next in your life.

If no one comes to mind. If sparkly glitter isn't falling around your head right now. If you're wondering if anyone will ever come along and invite you to take that next step in your life.

Let it be me.

Allow it to be me, right now, right here.

Grant me the joy of inviting you, of triggering you, to take action on this next step in your life.

The one that starts right now.

What if this book is your Larkin Street and I'm your John Muldoon?

Crazier things have been known to happen.

It might seem like nothing could move the mountain of your dream but what if it takes just a slight shiver of the earth to trigger the tiny earthquake that loosens the foundation just enough so the volcano that is your energy is allowed to erupt?

It might seem like nothing.

It might seem insignificant.

It might be perfectly and wonderfully **Seemingly Insignificant.**

It might be that your trigger happens right now.

Trigger Time Together

Even if you're thinking ahead to the "time" and you're happy to do it "together" with others, something has to flip the switch, change the channel, and get past the point of no return.

Trigger.

Repossible

- **Possible:** force the trigger yourself
- **Impossible:** wait to be 100% sure it's the right trigger
- **Repossible:** feel it, go with it

You can watch one of my favorite "Thursday Thunder" videos in the WBE Bonus Content, look for "Seemingly Insignificant" or here on YouTube: go.repossible.com/si.

9

TIME

THE PAST, PRESENT, AND FUTURE. WHICH DO
YOU HAVE CONTROL OVER?

> "Had the challenge been 3 weeks, I probably wouldn't
> have signed up."
>
> — S.S., WBE AUTHOR

The nutshell: a set amount of time and a deadline.

It's time for a quiz.

Which of the following inspires you to take action?

1. "The course schedule is extremely flexible! You can begin anytime you wish and you have access forever."
2. "It's a 12-month program with 52 weekly 1-on-1 calls and a 365-task checklist. If you don't finish in 365 days, your membership will automatically roll over into the next 365 days...but you'll have to start it all over."
3. "It's 10 days. We start May 1 and finish May 11. You'll have a book in your hands on May 11."

OK, fine, I'm playing it out a bit here but you get the idea.

Have you ever played email tag or phone tag with someone trying to set up a call or an appointment? It usually goes something like this:

> "How about next week?"
> "Sure."
> "Maybe Tuesday?"
> "Ooh, anything but Tuesday."
> "OK, Thursday?"
> "That's great. What time?"
> "10?"
> "Could we do afternoon?"

Are you tired yet?
Can we revert back to the quiz?

> "It's 10 days. We start May 1 and finish May 11. You'll have a book in your hands on May 11."

I'm one of the most flexible, casual, and low-key people I have ever met.

Yet I have learned the hard way that "someday" and "extended" and "flexible" have their downsides.

Remember John Muldoon on Larkin Street? He didn't say:

> "Hey Bradley, what if you started writing someday and wrote forever?"

> — NOT JOHN MULDOON

He said:

> "We're starting on the 1st of the month and going until the 30th. Write Every Day."

> — JOHN MULDOON

It starts, it ends, it has a deadline.

Trigger Time Together

You're already "triggered" but you need a timeframe, a deadline, you need to set that into your mind, your psyche, and your gut.
Time.

Repossible

- **Possible:** someday
- **Impossible:** yesterday
- **Repossible:** today

10

TOGETHER

YOU CAN GO IT ALONE BUT ASK THE OTHERS THIS: WHY?

"A thousand thanks for sticking with me. I was trying to cop out on joining the Tribe [online community], since I thought I needed to concentrate all my energy on simply writing this worst book. I have surrendered and filled out my profile. You are an awesome mentor for writers, a Pied Piper who can lead the way. God bless you!"

— S.P., WBE AUTHOR

So, you want to write a book?

Here you go. Here's how.

1. Write Book
2. Publish Book

That's it! You're done!

There are no secrets in this book (on how to write a book). You absolutely don't have to do it together with a group. You can just refer to those two items in the numbered list.

By the way, those two items are valid for both the "Worst Book Ever" and "Best Book Ever." Same roadmap, same steps.

Easy peasy.

I hear you. You're possibly saying:

> "Hey Bradley, I get the Trigger part, that's really important and then the Time bit, that sounds good, too. But then the Together thing? That's just optional, right?"

> — POSSIBLY YOU

Yep, let me set the record straight: **you can absolutely write a book alone.**

In fact, you have the steps and everything you need to get it done. Right here in this book.

There are just a few, let's see, what if we called them "Bonus Items" that we're missing out on when we go it solo.

I don't think I've had a numbered list for at least a few paragraphs.

Benefits of Together

1. Feedback
2. Input
3. Conversation
4. Friendship
5. Colleagues
6. Chatter
7. Discussion
8. Ideas other than your own
9. Experience
10. Shoulders (to lean on—or cry on)
11. Celebrating together
12. Sharing the wins

13. Softening the losses
14. Someone who "gets it" who "knows what you're going through"
15. Fun
16. Potential
17. The unexpected

I doubt that's an exhaustive list.

What might you think up for reasons to wanting to do it together?

Oh, might there be downsides? Feel like a list? I bet it will be shorter. But I won't hold back.

Downsides of Together

1. Negative feedback
2. Pushback
3. Arguments
4. Stewart smells like roast bell peppers
5. (Lack of) experience (or even, too much experience)
6. Personality clashes
7. Hildegard seems to be a witch
8. Baggage
9. The unknown

I'm sure there are loads more.

But #17 in the first list is actually all I need. In fact, if I had to sum it up, it's just that: **the unexpected.**

We pretty much know what's going to happen to our own selves. We know our thoughts, our capabilities, our dreams and desires.

But when you add more humans into the mix? It gets exponentially more interesting.

This one might seem like the one to skip but in reality, it's possibly the most powerful of them all.

Together.

Repossible

- **Possible:** go it alone
- **Impossible:** go it alone and reap the rewards of collaboration
- **Repossible:** we're better together

PART IV

MINDSET

10% FINGERS TO KEYBOARD. 90% IMAGINATION TO FINGERS.

"If you think you can do a thing or think you can't do a thing, you're right."

— HENRY FORD

11

NO GOAL, NO PURPOSE, NO MEANING

AUTHORS JUST WANT TO HAVE FUN

"Do you know what I realized after struggling with secretly turning my worst book ever into my best book ever? I realized that I never have fun for the sake of having fun anymore. Everything I do has to have a goal, a purpose, a meaning. And it's exhausting sometimes. Creating something that's not perfect or directly useful is fun (and is highly useful on another level) - and I haven't done that in a very long time. Thank you for doing this! I'm sure many people will get breakthroughs like this."

— NICOLINE HUIZINGA, WBE AUTHOR

One of the underlying philosophies of Worst Book Ever is to not take it too seriously, not to make it, secretly, into your Best Book Ever, and certainly not to take yourself too seriously.

As the WBE Author says above, what if this were just an exercise in fun? Remember being a kid? When they go to summer camp, are they supposed to learn how to tie nautical knots, study Spanish, and work on their interpersonal communications?

No, they're supposed to have fun.

Oops, they might learn those other things along the way, but what if the goal, the trophy, the finish line is to just have a good time?

Seriously.

No, wait.

Not seriously.

Yes, but seriously think about taking it not seriously.

OK, this chapter is clearly done because it's hard to make non-jokes about being overly serious about not being serious.

> **PRO TIP:** Just in case you've tilted your head like a curious and skeptical dog, remember I'm one of the most un-serious people I have ever met. This is also my 30th book in your hands. In other words, we can take ourselves less seriously and get "serious" stuff done.

Repossible

- **Possible:** pretend to have fun
- **Impossible:** force fun
- **Repossible:** relax, fail, enjoy

12

MATH QUIZ!

THIS WILL HURT YOU MORE THAN IT HURTS ME

> "If you can't explain it simply, you don't understand it well enough."
>
> — ALBERT EINSTEIN

It's time for a little simple—but powerful—math.

Let's take a few characteristics of the number 1 (as compared to the number 0).

The number 1:

1. Is larger than 0.
2. Can be multiplied by other numbers (zero multiplied by anything is always zero).
3. Is 100% closer to 2 than 0.
4. "Exists." The number 0 doesn't really exist. Show me zero apples. Show me zero books. They don't exist until we get to 1.

By definition, **because you now have a book:**

1. It is more than most people on the planet have ever written—or will ever write.
2. It makes you 100% closer to book #2 (remember, book zero "doesn't exist")
3. It's only your worst book until you write your next book.
4. It's also your best book—until you write your next book.
5. It's something you can hold in your hand (have fun trying to keep zero in your hand and showing it to someone ... "No, really, it's an idea, can't you see it?" #asylum)

Both of my kids, OK, fine, my wife, too, say they're terrible at math. But math is fun! Math helps us understand things like mindset! Math helps us finish our book.

What if it were easy?

1 is always greater than 0.

Always has been. Always will be.

Be the 1.

Repossible

- **Possible:** get started
- **Impossible:** hold your book idea in your hand
- **Repossible:** 1 kicks 0's butt

PART V

TOOLBOX

MEASURE TWICE, CUT ONCE

I'm pretty sure I have spent a total of 2 years, 37 days, and 14 hours (and counting ... wait, who's counting?) of my lifetime playing around with the software and tools I would eventually never use.

I want to save you some of your life.

13

THE DIY VERSION

HERE'S WHAT YOU NEED

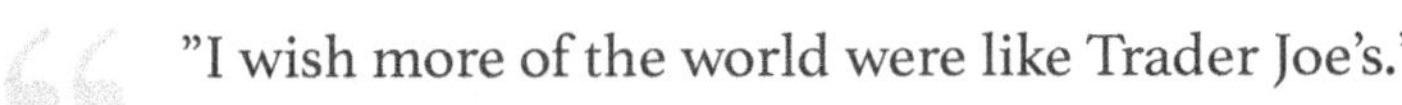

"I wish more of the world were like Trader Joe's."

— BRADLEY CHARBONNEAU

This section of the book is called Toolbox. As I've mentioned endlessly in this book, there's an accompanying 10-day, group, online challenge that you can optionally choose to join.

I want to make sure to provide you some value here in this book should you choose to not join us.

In the United States, there is a supermarket called Trader Joe's (little-known fact: it's owned by a German company that runs the bare-bones, products-on-a-wooden-pallet supermarket called ALDI in Europe). Of the many, many things I love about TJ's is that they have their own brands but not only that, they have just a small selection of choice.

I'm not in the U.S. as I write this (we moved to The Netherlands in 2016) so I can't go check right now but let's just pretend there are two types of peanut butter in TJ's.

1. Creamy
2. Crunchy

That's it. That's what you get. OK, OK, I know there are a few more. But in another U.S. supermarket, WalMart, there are, at last count, a gazillion different brands and styles and sizes and flavors and variations.

There are studies that show if you are given too much choice, often the result is you don't choose anything at all. Imagine half an aisle with just peanut butter. It can be so overwhelming, you could very possibly break out into a cold sweat and leave the store—without your peanut butter.

Or you waltz in Trader Joe's, where the staff wears Hawaiian shirts, and they have two choices:

1. Creamy
2. Crunchy

It's easy, right? It's easier.

We all have lots of knowledge. I know lots about writing, publishing, and marketing. My job, in my humble opinion, is not to send you to the WalMart of my mind but to the Trader Joe's.

I could easily overwhelm you with tools, software, subscriptions, podcasts, courses, books, and who-knows-what else but I'm going to don my Hawaiian shirt and give you fewer options, but researched, tried and true, and tested options.

I warn you because in the next chapter, I'm going to present you with (at least) 3 software tools.

Welcome to The Trader.

Repossible

- **Possible:** WalMart

- **Impossible:** choosing peanut butter
- **Repossible:** Trader Joe's

14

DO THIS NOT THAT

THE $10,000 CONSULTANT

 "Good judgment comes from experience, and experience comes from bad judgment."

— RITA MAE BROWN

A company hires a consultant to do a job. The consultant does the job and bills the company $10,000.

The company was happy with the work and fine with the price but asked for a more detailed invoice.

The consultant happily provided the invoice.

Consulting Job Detailed Invoice

1. $1 — Pressing the button that fixed the problem.
2. $9,999 — Knowing which button to press.

I've independently published 30 books (the one in your hands is my 30th) in 4 different series, I'm a part of at least half a dozen author Facebook groups, and I have tried, heard about, tested, and kicked to the curb all kinds of tools, tricks, gimmicks, strategies, programs, and software.

Rather than give you a choice, "Hey, here are 14 different tools you could use to __________, have fun figuring it out!" I'm just going to give you one (per service). If you want more, just ask. But more often than not, people tell me very directly:

> "Bradley, I don't want to make decisions and analyze and figure it out. Just tell me what to do."
>
> — YOU

This is now me Telling You What To Do

There are 3 services I'd like you to sign up for. I'm not going to get into detail about which one does what. I'm going to recommend you sign up for all 3. What we're really doing here is preparing for the Challenge before it starts and getting our ducks in a row.

These are all free.

1. Reedsy: This is where we'll be writing, organizing, and formatting our books.
2. Canva: Book cover design paradise (find the FREE account, you **don't need** the PRO account)
3. Prolific Works Our "distributor." Remember to sign up as an Author. (As of today, there is still a free option.)

In a nutshell, these three services are all you need to write, format, and publish your book.

I'll make links available to these services in the Bonus Content at go.repossible.com/wbe-bonus.

I'd love to hear how this goes. Drop a note in the comment area of the Bonus Content.

Remember Trader Joe's: these tools are all you need and they are all free (as of this writing).

All you need?

An idea.

A story.

Even better?
An idea with a story.

Repossible

- **Possible:** here are a bunch of options you may or may not understand
- **Impossible:** get experience without experiencing
- **Repossible:** here's what to do

P.S. I like both creamy and crunchy so I buy both.

15

THE ONE-WORD-LONG BOOK THAT WILL PROBABLY CHANGE YOUR LIFE

THIS WILL ONLY TAKE A SECOND…

"Miracles come in moments. Be ready and willing."

— WAYNE DYER

Just in case you weren't completely convinced that I, Mr. Author of this Book Guy, wasn't walking the talk, the day before our last WBE Challenge ended, I wrote a one-word book.

I even published it.

I wanted to show how easy it was to write a (ridiculously!) short book, give it a title, some love, format it properly with the tools I gave you, and put it up for sale (or give it away for free) in order to share your message, have your voice be heard, or just to prove that you could do it.

I present to you "The One-Word-Long Book that Will Probably Change Your Life."

You can find it in the bonus content at go.repossible.com/wbe-bonus.

"I READ IT IN ONE SITTING!"

THE ONE-WORD-LONG BOOK THAT WILL PROBABLY CHANGE YOUR LIFE

BRADLEY CHARBONNEAU

Repossible

- **Possible:** write a short book
- **Impossible:** think about having a great idea to write a one-word book but not doing it and then wishing you had done it and going back in time and have had done it
- **Repossible:** write a one-word book and not tell you, dear reader of this other book, what that one word is right here and right now

EPILOGUE

I wish I had this book, this challenge, this invitation when I was 21. Back when I was pretty sure my future was filled with fame and fortune and bright lights and big city.

Sure, well, it's been good.

But it would have been better had I dared "get over myself" and write a Worst Book Ever first.

Then I could have saved at least nine years of my life wondering who would be my trigger to live my dream.

AFTERWORD

Some of you might have been waiting for this chapter whispering to yourself, "See! I knew it! He's going to sell us something."

Here it is.

You see, I'm an artist at heart. A creator. Was it in the Rocky movie where he said, "I'm a lover not a fighter." Maybe it was Frozen ...

My business coach helps me to see it as I would have seen it back on Oct. 31, 2012: I would have welcomed the invitation to alter my life with open arms, a full heart, and an ocean of gratitude.

It is in that spirit in which I do want to formally invite you to join our next 10-Day "Write Your Worst Book Ever" Challenge.

The software I use for the online element of the courses allows me to create coupons. I get a creative kick out of using coupon code names that invoke a sense of the course.

For the WBE 10-Day challenge, in the spirit of this book and Larkin Street and John Muldoon and in my hopes that I might be the catalyst that propels you towards change and a deep sense of joy and meaning in your life, I offer you a 25% discount to the challenge by using the coupon code:

TRIGGER

You can read more about the challenge here:

go.repossible.com/wbe

Just like my upcoming book "You Don't Have to Write a Book," you have a choice. My role is to invite you, to show you a possible path, to be your trigger.

Should you choose to.

If you don't, I wish you well.

If you choose to join us, let's unlock your potential within.

ACKNOWLEDGMENTS

You.

Yep, you reading this book.

In the dedication, I dedicated this book to me of a certain date, October 31, 2012. That was the day before I started writing.

I acknowledge you, reading this book, about to partake on a journey that might be that day you look back on and remember that this was the day it started for you.

Remember, you might not, well, remember this is THE day. It might just seem like any other day but then you look back and you can pinpoint it to this day.

I dedicate, I acknowledge you, today, reading this book and about to write your own so that you can have your own dedication page and dedicate your book to the you of yesterday.

I also dedicate this book to the Worst Book Ever Alumni Authors who laughed, 1-star-reviewed, and wrote our first—and worst—books together.

You are rockstars.

ABOUT THE AUTHOR

This book was both painful and a joy to write.

Painful because I honest and truly wish I had had it when I started writing—or rather, started *not writing*.

A joy because it's out of me—and into you.

Writing is a big part of my life. Sure, I'm a speaker and a teacher, but writing the words down is my meditation, my surrender, my play, my joy, my meaning, my purpose, and my love.

I know I have a book called "You Don't Have to Write a Book" but in that book, I kind of say You Have to Write a Book *if you want to*.

While it's not the secret to all joy and happiness (actually, that secret is in the book called "The One-Word-Long Book that Will Probably Change Your Life"), I do believe "getting that book out of you" is a cleansing, cleaning, and purifying process.

It's a bit like jogging or going to the gym:

1. I don't often feel like going
2. I don't always love it when I'm there
3. But I usually get into a rhythm and it's good
4. I'm better off for having done it
5. I'm always glad I did it

I hope this little book has inspired you to put aside the pressures of perfection and let loose with some pathetically primitive prose.

Thanks for sharing your time with me.

I currently live in a little town in the woods outside of Utrecht in The Netherlands with my wife Saskia, famous two young boys of

"The Adventures of Li & Lu" fame, and our at-least-as-famous dog, Pepper.

This is my thirtieth book.

We're just getting started.

Find, ask, discuss, play, and dare at:
bradleycharbonneau.com

facebook.com/bradley.charbonneau.author
twitter.com/brathocha
instagram.com/brathocha
bookbub.com/profile/bradley-charbonneau
goodreads.com/bradleycharbonneau
amazon.com/author/bradleycharbonneau
linkedin.com/in/likoma
patreon.com/repossible
pinterest.com/likoma

ALSO BY BRADLEY CHARBONNEAU

Most of my books are also available as audiobooks (which I giddily narrate).
Search for my name at your favorite audiobook distributor, slip on your
headphones, and let me take you away.

Repossible

Who Will You Be Next?

1. Repossible
2. Every Single Day (+ Playbook)
3. Ask
4. Dare
5. Create (also available: Box Set #1)
6. Decide
7. Meditate
8. Spark (also available: Box Set #2)
9. Surrender
10. Play
11. Celebrate (also available: Box Set #3 and Box Set Complete)
12. Evaluate (2022)
13. Elevate (2022)
14. Give (2022)

Authorpreneur

Beyond the Book

1. You Don't Have To
2. How to Write Your Worst Book Ever

Charlie Holiday

The Chance is Yours

Short Trips

Just Put on the Shoes

Li & Lu

Bring Adventure Home

4. The Gift of Markree Castle
5. Driehoek (also available: Box Set)

Really Old ...

urban travel guide SAN FRANCISCO

THE END

You know what this really means, right?
It's just the beginning.
Trigger.